17 Prehistoric Agnathans

EVERYONE SHOULD KNOW ABOUT

STANTON F. FINK

VOLUME IV OF STANTON'S COLORING BOOKS

Acknowledgments

and Dedication

To my father, in whose books I discovered my first monsters.

To Will Caligan, whose help and encouragement is one of the primary reasons for this coloring book's existence.

To Mariano Silvera, who should have had his own artbooks

To Doctor David Morafka, who helped teach me to be more picky with my information.

To my friends, who helped push me to make this.

Table of Contents

Introduction

A "fish" is any vertebrate chordate that is not a tetrapod that can only breath air through lungs in one or more life stages (i.e., humans, other mammals, reptiles, their descendants, and most amphibians), or a descendant of a tetrapod that can only breath air through lungs (so we get the obligately aquatic amphibians and lungless salamanders).

A jawless fish, or agnathan, in turn, is any vertebrate chordate that isn't a gnathostome (i.e., not a tetrapod, bony fish, cartilaginous fish, acanthodian ora placoderm). But this begs the question, "what's a jaw?" A jaw is a bone derived from the first pair of gill arch-supports that were modified to help the first gnathostome to better inhale and exhale water through the gills. But, that is as far as this book will go, as it's about jawless fishes.

Glossary

- **Aquatic**- Living in water.
- **Agnathan**- Any vertebrate chordate that lacks anatomical jaws.
- **Arthropod**- Any member of the animal phylum Arthropoda, including trilobites, arachnids, crustaceans, insects, myriapods and their relatives. All arthropods have armor-like, jointed exoskeletons made of chitin-derived plates, sometimes reinforced with calcium carbonate, and jointed limbs.
- **Aspidine**- A hard tissue similar to bone tissue and dentine, but found only in the scales and armor of pteraspidomorph agnathans, and the scales of thelodonts.
- **Cambrian**- A period of time in the Paleozoic Era from 541 to 485 million years ago.
- **Carboniferous**- A period of time in the Paleozoic Era from 359 to 300 million years ago.
- **Cenozoic**- An era of time in the Phanerozoic Eon from 65 million years ago until now.
- **Chordate**- Any member of the animal phylum Chordata, including sea squirts, lancet fish, and vertebrates (such as lampreys, sharks, tuna, frogs, lizards, chickens, and people). All chordates have, at least at some point in their life cycle, a notochord, a long, flexible rod, usually made of cartilage, or, in the case of most vertebrates, cartilage and bone, running down the back from head to tail, directly beneath the neural tube.
- **Craniate**- Any vertebrate chordate that has a defined cranium or skull.
- **Cretaceous**- The last period of time in the Mesozoic Era, from 144 to 66 million years ago.
- **Devonian**- A period of time in the Paleozoic Era from 414 to 360 million years ago.
- **Fauna**- In an ecological context, "fauna" refers to the animal components of an ecosystem.
- **Formation**- In a geological or paleontological context, a formation is a group of rock layers.
- **Gnathostome**- A gnathostome is any vertebrate chordate with a moveable jaw (or had an ancestor with one).
- *__Incertae sedis__*- A Latin phrase literally meaning "uncertain seat." *"Incertae sedis"* is a term in classification used to refer to a species or group whose relationships with related organisms are unclear or poorly defined.
- **Mesozoic**- An era of time in the Phanerozoic Eon from 249 to 66 million years ago.
- **Mollusk**- Any member of the animal phylum Mollusca, including snails, clams, squid, octopuses, tusk shells and chitons. Most mollusks have a calcium carbonate shell, and a toothed, file-like tongue called a radula. All mollusks have a cape-like organ, the mantle, which usually secretes the shell, and houses breathing organs, and a nervous system.
- **Nekton**- Any aquatic animal that lives either entirely or almost entirely in the water column, and relies on its own swimming or propulsion abilities to keep and move itself

in and around the water column. Anchovies, porpoises and ichthyosaurs are examples of nekton.

- **Neogene**- The second third of the Cenozoic Era, comprising of the Miocene and the Pliocene periods.
- **Ordovician**- A period of time in the Paleozoic Era from 484 to 440 million years ago.
- **Paleozoic**- An era of time in the Phanerozoic Eon from 249 to 66 million years ago.
- **Pharynx**- A structure in the throat of many animals located directly behind the mouth or oral chamber. In vertebrates, it often houses breathing structures, like gills.
- **Plankton**- An organism that uses water currents and waterflow to as its primary means of transportation in the water column because it is either too small to move long distances by its own power, or lacks the ability to propel itself entirely. Sargassum seaweed and jellyfish are two varieties of plankton.
- **Terrestrial**- Living on land.

Name	Sea Spriggan
Species	*Metaspriggina walcotti*
Phylum	Chordata
clade	Craniata
Size	Up to 10 centimeters in length
Time Period	Middle Cambrian, about 505 million years ago.
Location	British Columbia: Holotype found in the Walcott Quarry in Burgess Shale, more specimens found in the Marble Canyon in Kootenay National Park.
Comments	When the first two fossils of the Sea Spriggan, *Metaspriggina walcotti*, were origin discovered, it was originally thought to be a descendant of the Precambrian "maybe-an-arthropod" *Spriggina*, but then the holotype was then understood to be of a poorly preserved chordate similar to the cephalochordate, the Urfisch, *Pikaia gracilens* (the smaller animal in the picture here). In 2012-2013, 44 more fossils, this time exquisitely preserved, were found in Marble Canyon Quarry of Kootenay National Park. These fossils showed that the sea spriggan was a primitive craniate, that is, a chordate with a defined head region, with modern-day craniates including hagfish, lampreys, and jawed fishes, including their descendants the tetrapods (i.e., from coelacanths to humans).

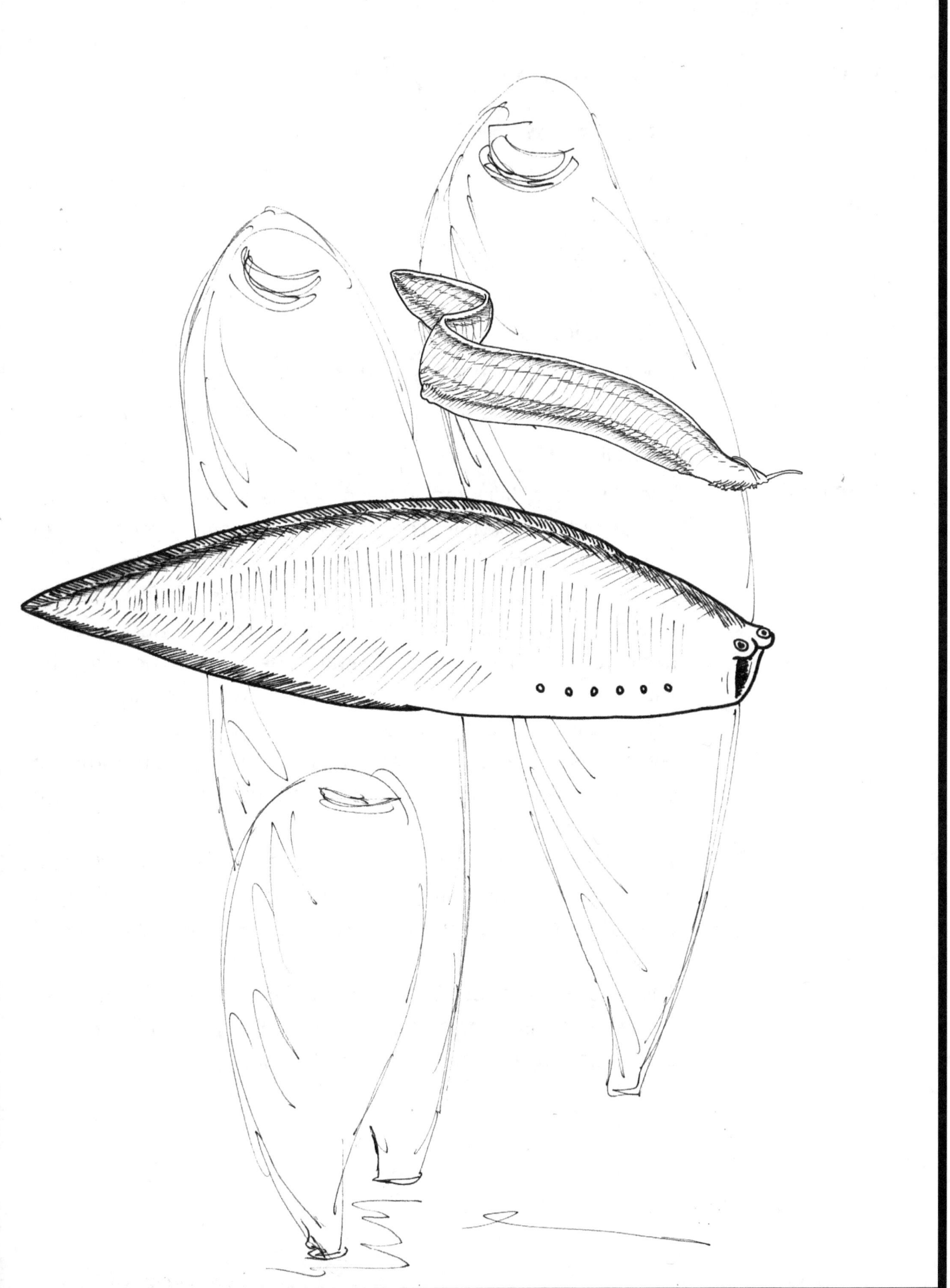

Name	Wyoming Wishing Starfish
Species	*Astraspis desiderata*
Phylum	Chordata
Subphylum	Vertebrata
Class	Pteraspidomorphi
Subclass	Astraspida
Order	Astraspidiformes
Size	Up to 20 centimeters in length
Time Period	Middle to Late Ordovician, from 467 to 443 million years ago
Location	Wyoming, United States of America
Comments	The Wyoming Wishing Starfish, *Astraspis desiderata*, is one of the oldest unequivocal vertebrates known from more or less whole-body fossils found in Ordovician-aged marine strata in the US state of Wyoming. These fossils show a tadpole-shaped, slit-mouthed animal covered in bony scales made of the tissues aspidine and dentine. The way the aspidine was used to form the scale is diagonistic of a typical pteraspidomorph, a member of a class of armored jawless fishes, and represents a period in pteraspidomorph evolution before the scales fused together in adults to form exoskeleton-like armor.

The genus name, *Astraspis*, translates as "star-shield," and refers to how the outer surface of each scale is made of aspidine, and is covered in little star-like bumps made of dentine.

The related species, the Bolivian Resplendent Starfish, *A. resplendens*, is known from scales found in Middle to Late Ordovician-aged marine strata of Bolivia.

Name	Cowiekipper
Species	*Cowielepis ritchiei*
Phylum	Vertebrata
Class	Anaspida
Order	Birkeniida
Family	*Incertae sedis*
Size	At least 10 centimeters long
Time Period	Late Wenlock to Early Ludlow epochs of the Middle Silurian, about 430 to 425 million years ago
Location	The Cowie Harbour fish beds of Stonehave, Scotland
Comments	The Cowiekipper, *Cowielepis ritchiei*, is, relatively speaking, a recently described anaspid from Middle Silurian Scotland. It displays a unique combination of traits otherwise unique to other anaspids. This unique combination of anaspid characteristics show that, within the anaspid order Birkeniida, the cowiekipper is closely related to the anaspids *Pharyngolepis*, *Pterygolepis,* and *Rhyncholepis*.
	Lifestyle-wise, however, it probably very similar to other anaspids, swimming in the water column using side-to-side undulations of both the body, and sucking up plankton.

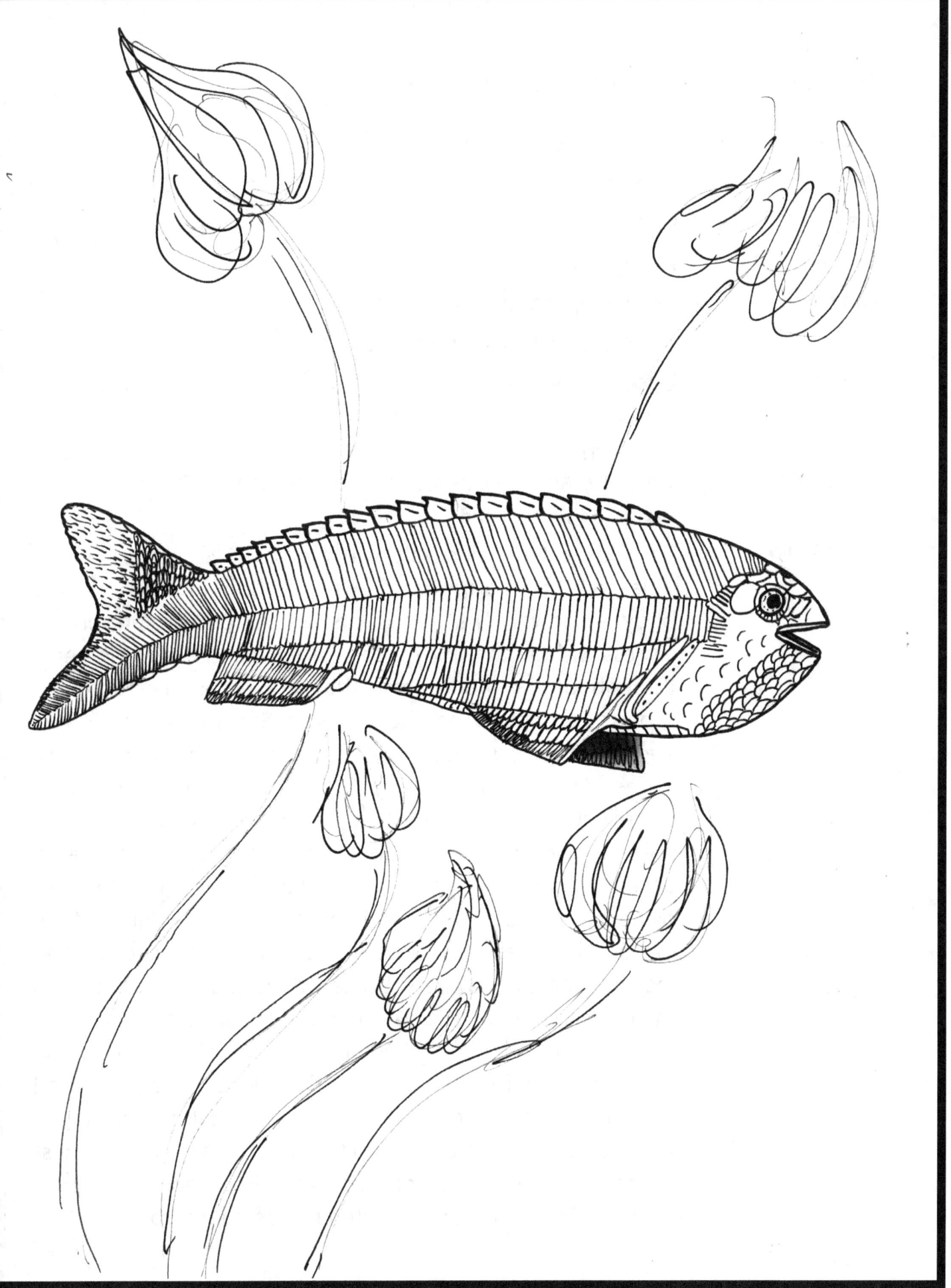

Name	Topscaled Sharkpole
Species	*Archipelepis turbinata*
Phylum	Chordata
Class	Thelodonti
Order	Archipelepidida
Family	Archipelepididae
Size	Up to 6 or 7 centimeters in length
Time Period	Upper Llandovery to Lower Wenlock epochs of the Early Silurian, 434 to 432 million years ago
Location	Avalanche Lake in the Mackenzie Mountains of the Yukon Territory, and Baillie-Hamilton Island in the Canadian Arctic Archipelago, Canada

Comments

The Topscaled Sharkpole, *Archipelepis turbinata*, is the oldest and most primitive known thelodont in which a whole body is known. The thelodonts are a group of "armorless" jawless fishes that were found in marine environments throughout the world from the Late Ordovician until the group's extinction at the end of the Devonian period. Thelodont scales superficially resemble the microscopic scales that make up shark shagreen, but differ profoundly in the structure and tissue makeup. Even so, some researchers mistake Ordovician thelodont scales for those of sharks. Because thelodont scales were weakly attached to their owners, were constantly shed and replaced throughout their owners' lifetimes, and were unique to specific species and locations on their owners' bodies, thelodont scales are used by geologists to date various Middle Paleozoic strata.

The topscaled sharkpole had spinning top-shaped scales on its back. Unlike most other thelodonts, the topscaled sharkpole had no fins other than the caudal, having yet to evolved any. The internal structure of its scales also suggest it represents what thelodonts were like soon after they diverged from the closely related pteraspidomorphs.

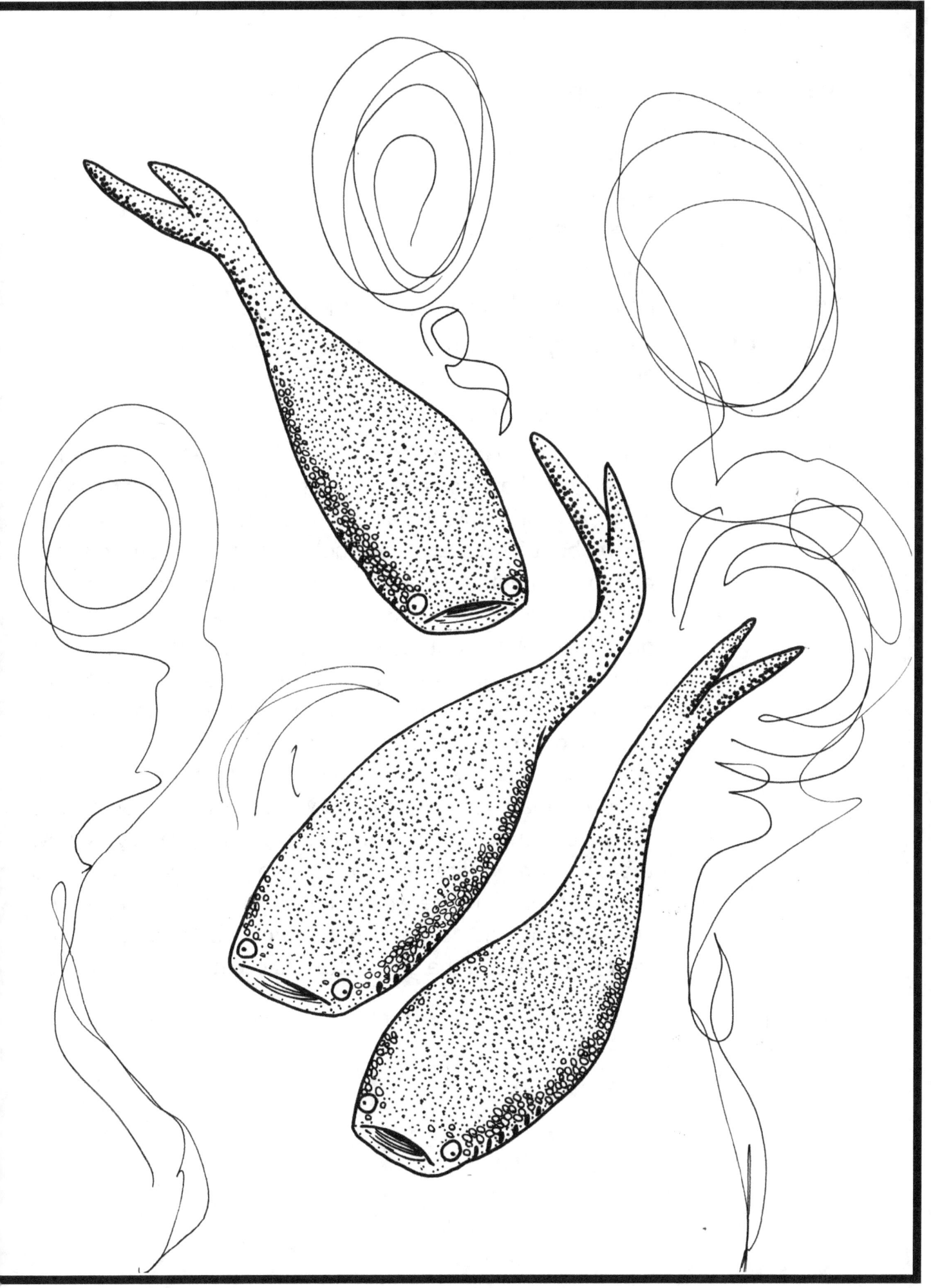

Name	Jamprey
Species	*Jamoytius kerwoodi*
Phylum	Chordata
Class	Hyperoartia
Order	Jamoytiiformes
Size	Maybe up to 10 centimeters in length
Time Period	Llandovery Epoch of the Silurian, 444 to 428 million years ago
Location	County of Lanarkshire, Scotland
Comments	The Jamprey, *Jamoytius kerwoodi*, is a mysterious, eel-like jawless fish that has undergone many, many transformations in its perception by humans, at least, by those humans who know about it, ever since the holotype, a squished front-half of a long something-or-other was discovered and described by Errol White in 1946. When the jamprey was first discovered, White touted it as "the most primitive vertebrate ever." Later, the jamprey was then reappraised as a primitive, elongated anaspid with long, undulating pectoral fins that ran along almost the entire length of its body. In 2010, it was realized these "fins" were actually portions of the bodywall that were pinched outward when the corpse was squished during burial. Since 2010, the jamprey is now thought to be a filter-feeding relative of the lampreys, and represents a link between lampreys on one end and anaspids, thelodonts, pteraspidomorphs, osteostracans, and their relatives, and the gnathostomes on the other.

Name	Coinscaled Sharkpole
Species	*Thelodus parvidens*
Phylum	Chordata
Class	Thelodonti
Order	Thelodontiformes
Family	Coleolepididae
Size	Estimated to be up to one meter in length
Time Period	From Late Llandovery epoch of the Early Silurian until probably the Ludlow epoch of the Late Silurian, from about 435 until 424 million years ago
Location	England, Wales, and Eastern Canada
Comments	Many of the body scales of the Coinscaled Sharkpole, *Thelodus parvidens,* approach the size of an American quarter (that is, have an average diameter of 24 to 25 millimeters). If one compares these to more normal-sized thelodonts, and, no pun intended, scale up the scales' former owners, the coinscaled sharkpole would have probably been about one meter in length, and would have been one of the largest vertebrates during the entire Silurian period, only equaled in size by the megajawed sarcopterygian, *Megamastax amblyodus*, of Late Silurian China, which may have also been about one meter long.
	The scales of the coinscaled sharkpole are found in Early to Late Silurian sites in Eastern Canada and Great Britain, suggesting that the coinscaled lived in a narrow sea that was flanked on either side by lands that would eventually become Eastern Canada and Great Britain. The coinscaled's large size would have made swimming across this sea fairly easy.

Name	Phialfish
Species	*Phialaspis symmondsi*
Phylum	Chordata
Class	Pteraspidomorphi
Subclass	Heterostraci
Order	Traquairaspidiformes
Family	Traquairaspididae
Size	About 2 to 3 centimeters from "wingtip to wingtip"
Time Period	Late Silurian to Early Devonian, about 420 to 416 million years ago
Location	Wales and England
Comments	The (Symmonds') Phialfish, *Phialaspis symmondsi* (also *Traquairaspis symmondsi*), is a tiny heterostracan fish from marine environments of Wales and England, living during the Late Silurian until sometime during the Early Devonian. The phialfish belongs to a specific group of heterostracans called the "traquairaspids," and most tended to look very much like almonds, or sesame seeds with tails, and sometimes dorsal spines on the top. The phialfish, in contrast, resemble jets or paper airplanes (with tails) due to large, extended branchial plates around the exit-opening of its gills. These wing-like branchial plates, coupled with a flattened, but upturned, nose-like rostral plate strongly suggest that the phialfish either spent a great deal of time in the water column off of the seafloor, or could get off of the seafloor and into the water column in a hurry if it wanted to.

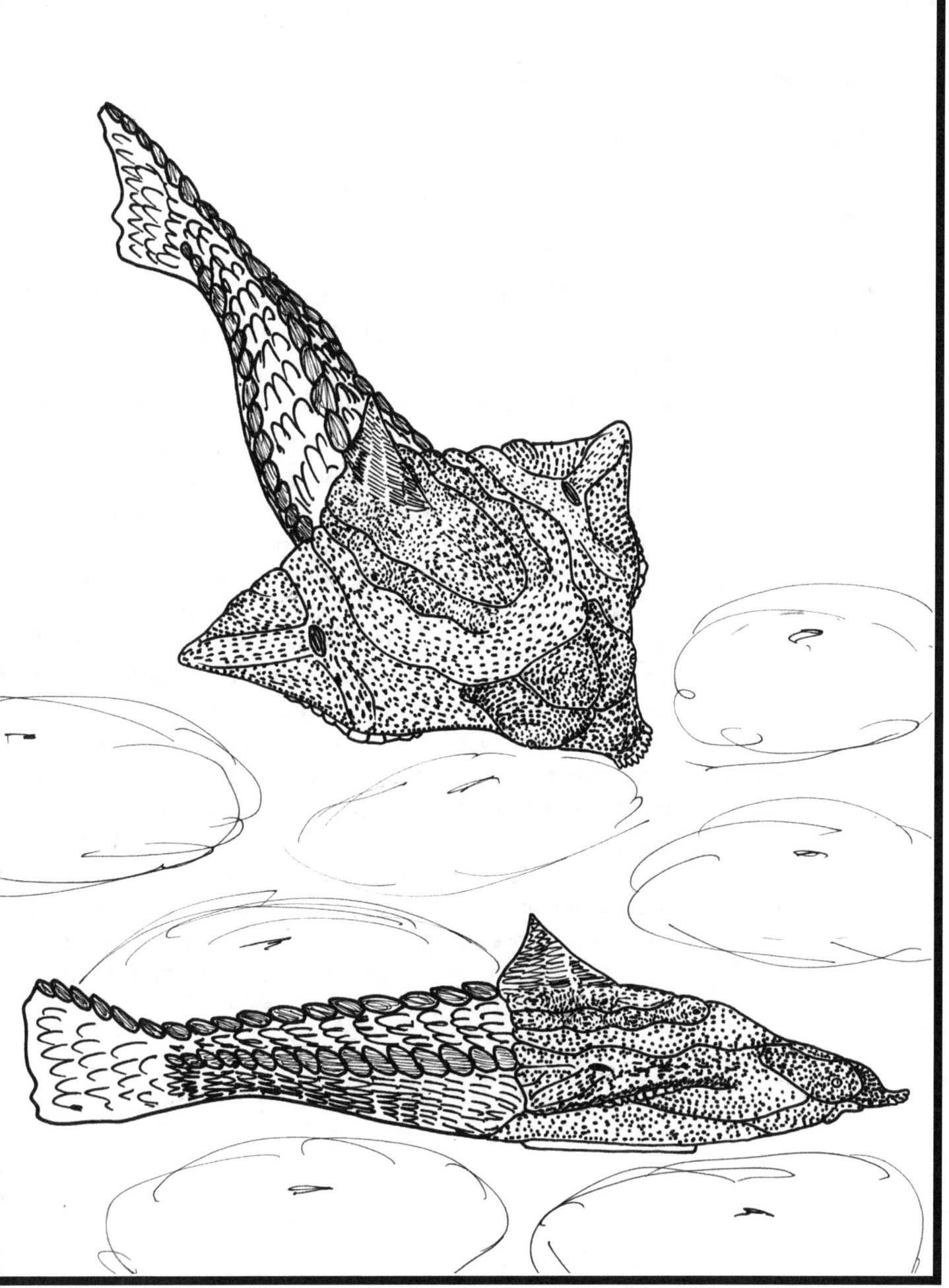

Name	Shankou Kuiyu
Species	*Sinogaleaspis shankouensis*
Phylum	Chordata
Class	Galeaspida
Order	Eugaleaspidiformes
Size	Head shield about two centimeters wide
Time Period	Late Wenlock epoch of the Middle Silurian, about 429 to 427 million years ago
Location	Xikeng/Xitun Formation of Northern Jiangxi Province, China.
Comments	The Shankou Kuiyu, or Shankou helmet fish, *Sinogaleaspis shankouensis*, is a typical member of Galeaspida, an extinct class of jawless fishes entirely restricted to marine and estuarine environments of what are now China and Vietnam, back when the Sino-Chinese/Vietnamese region was an island continent during the Silurian and Devonian periods.

All galeaspids can be identified by the fused head-shield, and the enormous, mouth-like nostril that used to force water in through a maze-like series of gills. Although the galeaspids look very much like cyathaspid heterostracans, the galeaspids are actually more closely related to the osteostracans due to comparisons of gill and cranium anatomies.

Fossils of the shankou kuiyu are found in marine strata of the Xikeng or Xitun Formation, in the northern region of Jiangxhi Province. In life, the shankou kuiyu probably swam near the bottom of shallow-water marine environments, slurping and nibbling detritus from the sediment.

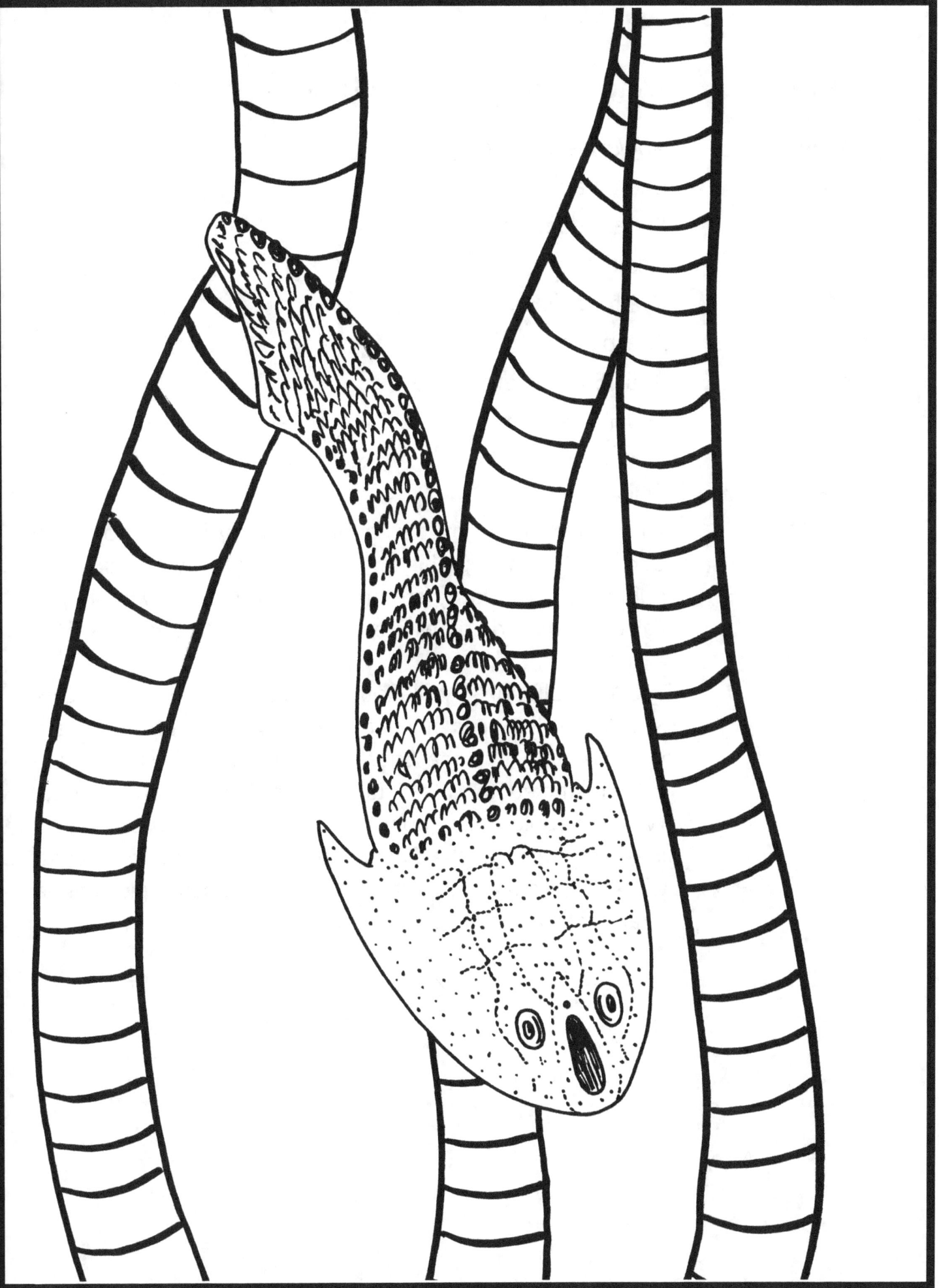

Name	MacCullough's Anglafisch
Species	*Anglaspis macculloughi*
Phylum	Chordata
Class	Pteraspidomorphi
Subclass	Heterostraci
Order	Cyathaspidida
Family	Ariaspidae
Size	9 to 15 centimeters long
Time Period	Pridoli Epoch of the Late Silurian Period, about 423 million years ago
Location	Wales
Comments	The Anglafisches of the genus *Anglaspis* are popularly portrayed in prehistoric reconstructions as the quintessential, heavily armored heterostracan, swimming in Paleozoic seas, doing whatever it is heterostracans did when alive. The MacCullough's Anglafisch, *A. macculloughi*, is from Late Silurian shallow seas in what is now Wales, and represents a typical member of the British dynasty of anglafisches, who were restricted to Late Silurian-aged British marine strata. When people talk about "Devonian *Anglaspis*," they invariably refer to the Spitzbergen lineage of anglafisches, whose fossils are found in the Early Devonian-aged marine strata of the island of Spitzbergen.

Name	Schmidt's Pirukad
Species	*Tremataspis schmidtii*
Phylum	Chordata
Class	Osteostraci
Order	Thyestiida
Family	Tremataspididae
Size	Head-shield average length of 3 centimeters
Time Period	Ludlow epoch of the Middle Silurian, 423 to 421 million years ago
Location	Saaremaa Estonia
Comments	Schmidt's Pirukad, *Tremataspis schmidtii,* is one of several thyestiid osteostracans that lived and burrowed in sandy lagoon bottoms in what is now the island of Saarema, Estonia. From the top, Schmidt's pirukad (one of several species of pirukad) would have looked something like a modern horseshoe crab with a long, swishing scaley tail. Pirukads would have had a collective lifestyle similar to horseshoe crabs, in that they would have burrowed through the sediment, though, rather than use legs, a pirukad would have used its tail to thrust its head-shield forward in the sand.
	Pirukads, much like their relatives in the genus *Thyestes,* would have eaten detritus and other organic matter in the sand, sucked up with a small mouth at the very front of the head-shield.

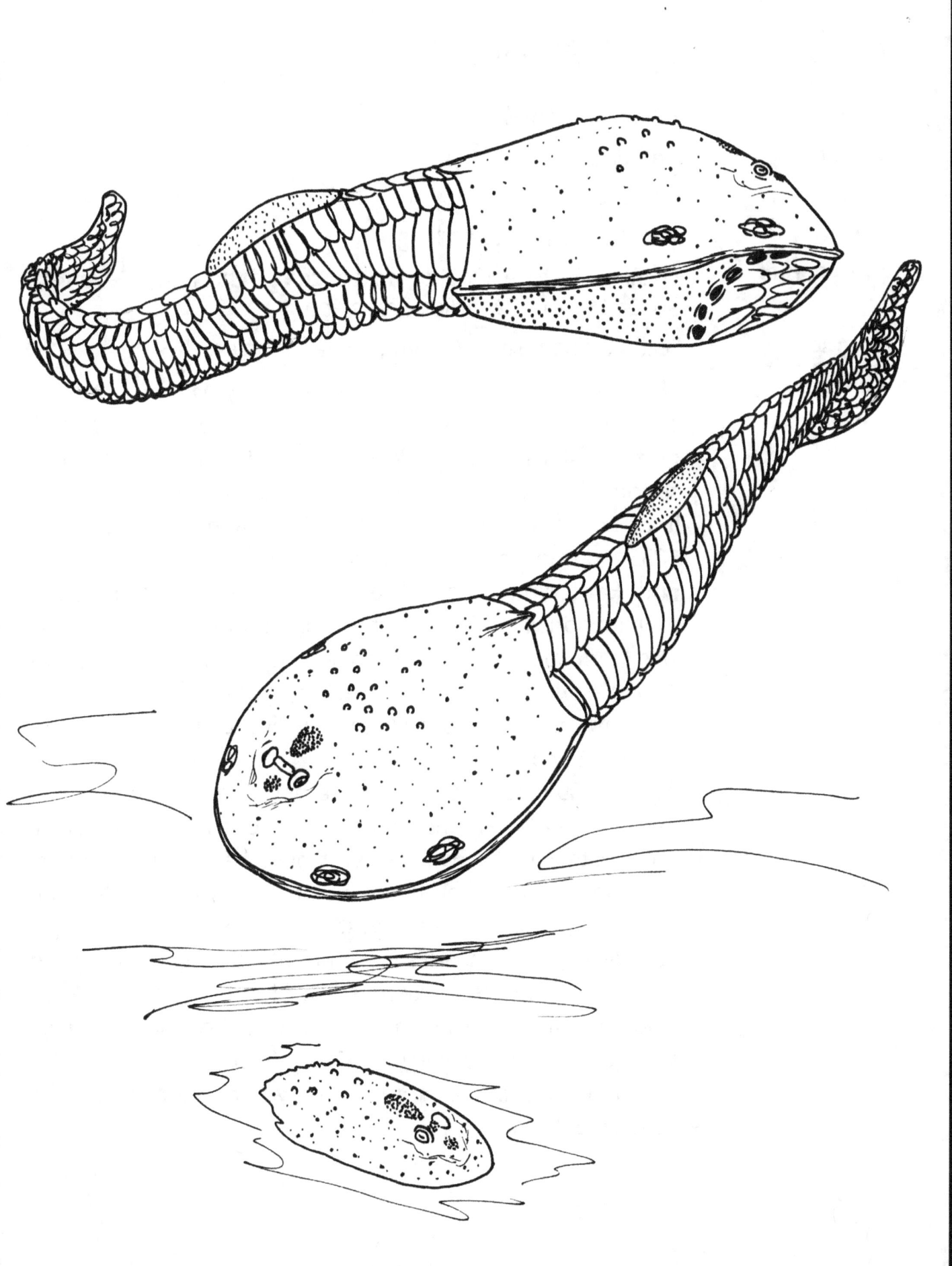

Name	Lyell's Headfish
Species	*Cephalaspis lyelli*
Phylum	Chordata
Class	Osteostraci
Size	About 30 centimeters long
Time Period	Lochkovian to early Pragian epochs of the Early Devonian, about 412 to 409 million years ago
Location	"Old Red Sandstone" of England and Wales
Comments	The (Sir Charles) Lyell's Headfish, *Cephalaspis lyelli*, is simultaneously the best known and most overlooked of all of the osteostracan jawless fishes. Soon after the first specimen was discovered by Sir Charles Lyell, who then gave it to the illustrious geologist Louis Agazzis to describe in 1835, no one else apparently bothered to study the species until Errol White and Erik Stensiö made a more thorough examination in 1958. Further compounding the situation was the fact that researchers kept using the genus *Cephalaspis* as a waste-basket taxon to hold any osteostracan that looked remotely like Lyell's headfish for literally over a century.

As of a 2009 study, *C. lyelli* is the only species confirmed to be in *Cephalaspis*, and represents the sister group of all other osteostracans who have or once had defined corners on their head-shields, including the Zenaspids, the Benneviaspidids, and the Thyestiids.

Ecologically, the headfish is thought to have ploughed through sediment of estuaries in order to sift and suck up edible detritus with its small mouth at the front tip of its shovel-like head-shield. The headfish sensed its environment primarily through nerve-rich patches on the head-shield.

Name	Sichelfisch
Species	*Drepanaspis gemuendenensis*
Phylum	Chordata
Class	Pteraspidomorphi
Order	Pteraspidiformes
Suborder	Psammosteida
Family	Psammosteidae
Size	Ranging from 9.5 to 68.5 centimeters in length
Time Period	Emsian epoch of the Early Devonian, about 405 to 400 million years ago
Location	Hunsrück Slate lagerstätte of Southwestern Germany
Comments	The Sichelfisch, *Drepanaspis gemuendenensis* is the best known of all psammosteid heterostracan fishes, because of the numerous (mostly) complete specimens found from the Hunsrück Slate. These specimens include both small juveniles and very large adults.

During the Emsian, what would become the Hunsrück Mountains was the muddy bottom of an estuary which received an almost constant rain of plant matter washed down from the river's mouth. This place supported a diverse community of echinoderms, arthropods, some fish and mollusks.

The sichelfisch swam around at the bottom in order to force water through its characteristically wide mouth and past its gills, and, in the process, filter-feed on organic particles and planktonic organisms. This lifestyle would be shared with all other psammosteids.

Of course, life was not all starfish and roses for the sichelfisch: while no fossils show suggestions of predation, researchers do know why there are so many exceptionally preserved fossils in the Hunsrück Slate, in that there were numerous oxygen-free, or "anoxic" zones where all aerobic organisms that entered them would immediately suffocate and die, and be then be covered in sulfur-reducing bacteria, and then mud before the corpses completely disintegrated.

Name	Kiangyou Lungmen Kuiyu
Species	*Lungmenshanaspis kiangyouensis*
Phylum	Chordata
Class	Galeaspida
Order	Huananaspidiformes
Family	Huanaspidae
Subfamily	Macrothyraspinae
Size	About 8 centimeters wide, from point to point
Time Period	Pragian Epoch of the Early Devonian, from 410 until 407 million years ago
Location	Eastern Tibetan Plateau, Southeastern China and Northern Vietnam
Comments	The Kiangyou Lungmen Kuiyu, or Kiangyou Dragon's Gate Helmetfish, *Lungmenshanaspis kiangyouensis*, in the learned opinion of paleoichthyologist John Long, possesses one of the most bizarre vertebrate skulls known. The Kiangyou lungmen kuiyu, which is named for the Lungmen Mountains, has a long, needle-like rostrum, and two perpendicularly positioned, recurved lateral spines. These appendages may have helped better adjust and stabilize the animal's hydrodynamics during swimming.
	Despite such enigmatic extravagance, the dragon's gate helmetfish probably had a lifestyle very similar to other galeaspids, filter-feeding while competing with the local, indigenous endemic antiarch placoderms.

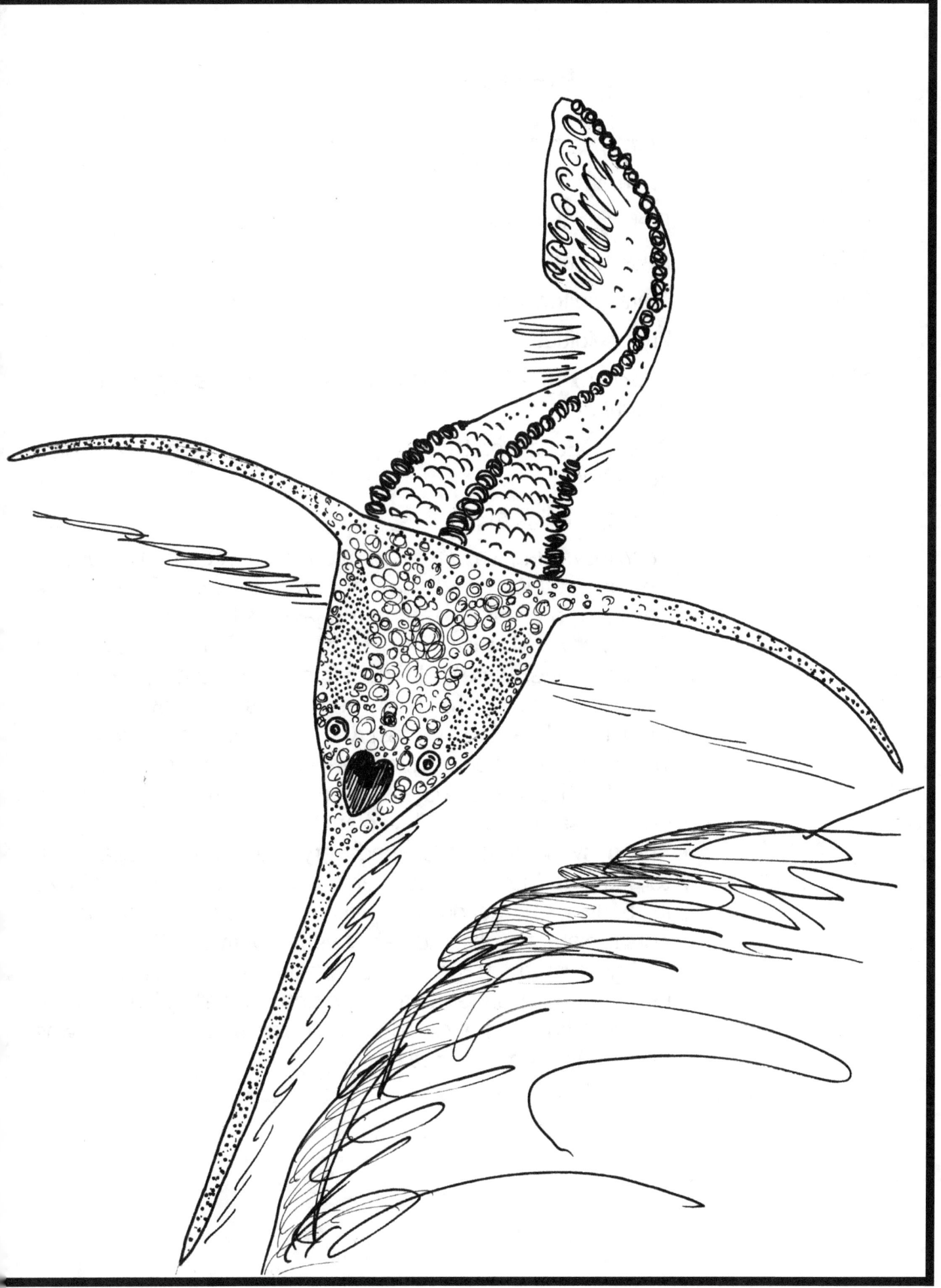

Name	Nosy Wingfish
Species	*Pteraspis rostrata*
Phylum	Chordata
Class	Pteraspidomorphi
Subclass	Heterostraci
Order	Pteraspidiformes
Family	Pteraspididae
Size	About 15 to 20 centimeters from tip of rostrum to end of caudal fin
Time Period	Pragian Epoch of the Early Devonian, 410 to 407 million years ago
Location	England, Belgium
Comments	The Nosy Wingfish, *Pteraspis rostrata*, is regarded as one of the archetypical heterostracan, and is one of the more popular representative "armored jawless fishes." The nosy wingfish, as with all other members of Pteraspididae, were nekton that swam in the upper water column in order to filter-feed on shoals of plankton. Numerous fossils that preserve the lower lip show that it was made up of several, finger-like plates that would have modified the flow of water through the mouth, apparently in order to selectively swallow plankton of specific sizes. The nosy wingfish is shaped very much like a bullet or a torpedo, and its branchial plates extend out to help stabilize its body. A large dorsal spine at the anterior end of the dorsal plate also helped with hydrodynamics. The rostrum had grooves on its underside to help direct water both into its mouth and underneath its ventral or belly plate. While the front half was encased in bony plates, the back half was covered in prominent scales.

Name	Visionfish
Species	*Pituriaspis doylei*
Phylum	Chordata
Class	Pituriaspida
Size	Head-shield is about 4.5 centimeters long.
Time Period	Givetian Epoch of the Middle Devonian, 390 million years ago
Location	Georgina Basin of western Queensland, Australia.
Comments	When Gavin Young discovered the first fossil of the visionfish, *Pituriaspis doylei*, or, rather, understood what was inside the empty sandstone cast, he found the remains of a fish so strange, he thought he was in a vision-quest caused by an aborigine hallucinogen called "pituri."

The visionfish, *Pituriaspis doylei*, had a massive head-shield that resembled a tunic, covering its thorax, and had openings behind the eyes for gills, and shoulder-like openings for the pectoral fins. So far, the visionfish, the related *Neeyambaspis*, and (most of) the osteostracans are the only known agnathans that have pectoral fins similar to those of gnathostomes. The most remarkable feature of the visionfish is its long, nose-like rostrum, the function of which remains unknown.

The visionfish lived together with *Neeyambaspis*, and arthrodire placoderms of the genus *Wutagoonaspis* in an estuary where the Georgina Basin is today, in western Queensland, Australia.

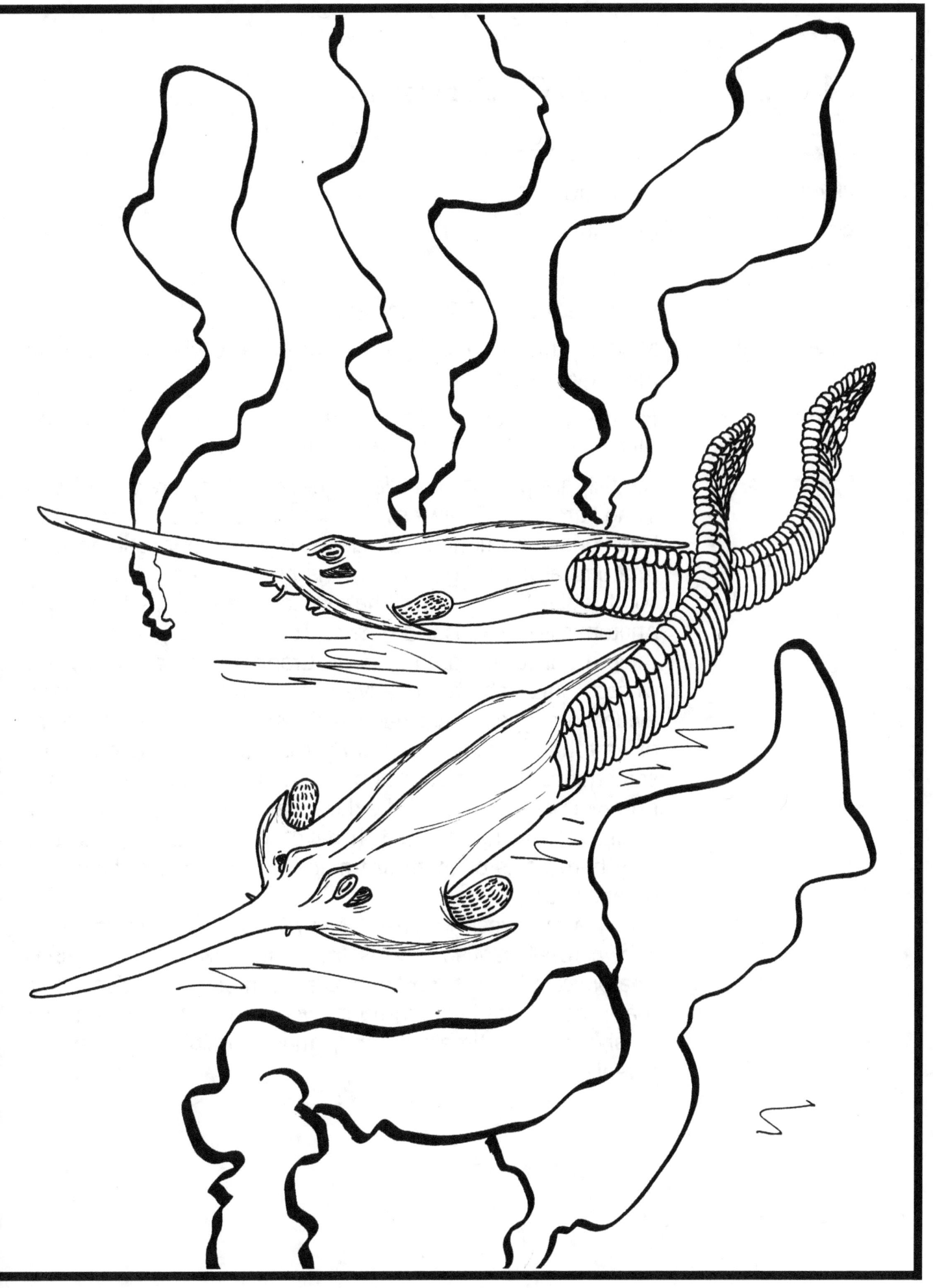

Name	Mazon Creek Hagfish
Species	*Myxinikela siroka*
Phylum	Chordata
clade	Craniata
Class	Myxini
Size	Only specimen is 7.2 centimeters long
Time Period	Middle Pennsylvanian Epoch of the Late Carboniferous, 300 million years ago
Location	Francis Creek Shale, Carbondale Formation of Will County, Illinois, USA. Part of the Mazon Creek Lagerstätte.
Comments	Hagfish are peculiar chordates: because they are one of two living groups of jawless "fishes," they have long been traditionally thought of as close relatives of the lampreys. Anatomically, and genetically, hagfish are not vertebrates, so, they actually aren't that closely related to lampreys. Anatomically, hagfish do have (cartilaginous) skulls, and thus, are in the chordate group Craniata, and are thus, the closest invertebrate relatives of vertebrates. Genetic evidence suggests that hagfish diverged from the ancestors of vertebrates sometime during the Cambrian period, 500-something million years ago. The only fossils of hagfish, however, date back to the late Carboniferous. This isn't terribly surprising, as hagfish have no bone tissue, and the only hard parts of them are made of keratin, which readily deteriorates.

The Mazon Creek Hagfish, *Myxinikela siroka*, is the first known fossil hagfish, and is from the Mazon Creek Fauna. Anatomically, it is almost identical to modern hagfish, save that it has (for a hagfish) huge eyes. The only known fossil is about 7 centimeters, and, may possibly represent a juvenile.

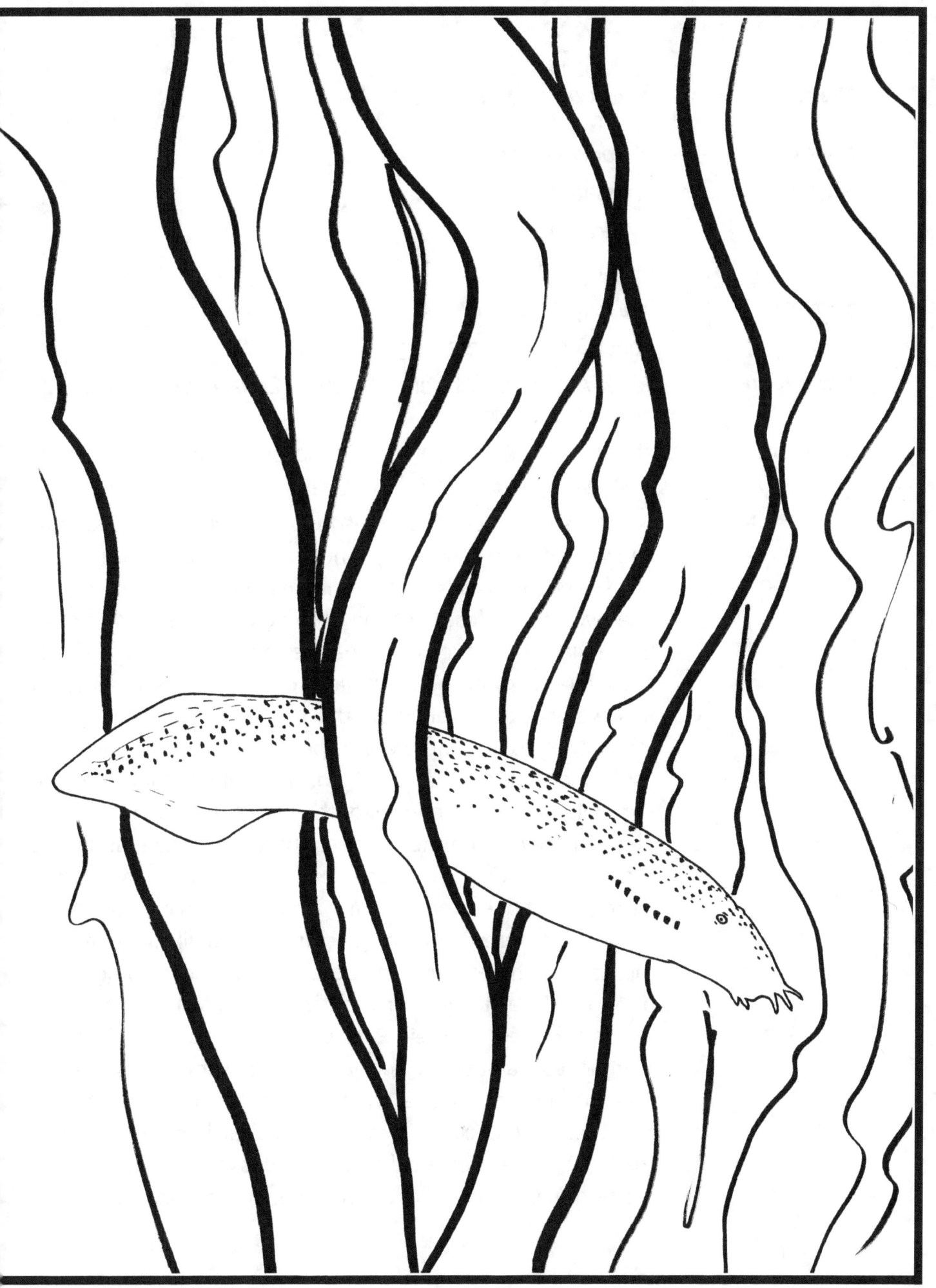

Name	Mesozoic Lamprey
Species	*Mesomyzon mengae*
Phylum	Chordata
Class	Hyperoartii
Order	Petromyzontiformes
Family	Petromyzontidae
Size	About 8 centimeters long
Time Period	Early Aptian Epoch of the Early Cretaceous Period, 125 million years ago.
Location	Yixian Formation, Lower Cretaceous; Ningcheng, Inner Mongolia, China
Comments	The Mesozoic Lamprey, *Mesomyzon mengae*, is the only known lamprey, and only known agnathan known from post-Paleozoic fossils (two specimens in this case).

The two known fossils of the Mesozoic lamprey come from the Yixian Formation in what is now Ningcheng, Inner Mongolia of China. The Yixian Formation was a series of freshwater lakes in are now the provinces of Liaoning and Inner Mongolia that were repeatedly filled by volcanic ashfalls over the course of 11 or so million years from the Barremian to Aptian epochs of the Early Cretaceous.

The anatomy of the mesozoic lamprey is largely identical to those of adult modern lampreys of the family Petromyzontidae, though, *M. mengae* is very small by modern lamprey standards. It was unlikely that the mesozoic lamprey was carnivorous or blood-feeding, as it did not appear to have any teeth like carnivorous lampreys, such as the sea lamprey, *Petromyzon marinus*. Because the ammocoete larvae of living lampreys do not tolerate warm temperatures or tropical climates, the mesozoic lamprey's presence in the Yixian Formation adds further evidence that these lakes were in a cold climate, possibly comparable to modern Alaska, but with defined wet and dry seasons.

Bibliography

- Amiot, R.; Wang, X.; Zhou, Z.; Xiaolin Wang, X.; Buffetaut, E.; Lécuyer, C.; Ding, Z.; Fluteau, F.; Hibino, T.; Kusuhashi, N.; Mo, J.; Suteethorn, V.; Yuanqing Wang, Y.; Xu, X.; Zhang, F. (2011). "Oxygen isotopes of East Asian dinosaurs reveal exceptionally cold Early Cretaceous climates". *Proceedings of the National Academy of Sciences*. **108** (13): 5179–5183.

- Bardack, D. 1991. First fossil hagfish (Myxinoidea): a record from the Pennsylvanian of Illinois. Science, 254: 701–703

- Blieck, Alain. "Les Hétérostracés Ptéraspidiformes, Agnathes du Silurien-Dévonien du Continent nord-atlantique et des blocs avoisinants: révision systématique, phylogénie, biostratigraphie, biogéographie." (1984).

- Blom, Henning. "A new anaspid fish from the Middle Silurian Cowie Harbour fish bed of Stonehaven, Scotland." Journal of Vertebrate Paleontology 28.3 (2008): 594-600.

- Chang, M. M.; Zhang, J.; Miao, D. (2006). "A lamprey from the Cretaceous Jehol biota of China". *Nature*. **441** (7096): 972–974.

- Conway Morris, Simon (March 2008). "A Redescription of a Rare Chordate, *Metaspriggina walcotti* Simonetta and Insom, from the Burgess Shale (Middle Cambrian), British Columbia, Canada". *Journal of Paleontology*. Boulder, CO: The Paleontological Society. **82** (2): 424–430.

- Forey, P. L., and Janvier, P. (1993). Agnathans and the origin of jawed vertebrates. *Nature*, 361, 129-134.

- Fredholm, Doris. "Agnathan vertebrates in the lower Silurian of Gotland, Sweden." *GFF* 112.1 (1990): 61-80.

- Groh, Selina. "Patterns of diversification in osteostracan evolution." (2014).

- Janvier, Philippe. (1993). Patterns of diversity in the skull of jawless fishes. In *The Skull* (ed. J. Hanken and B. K. Hall), Vol. 2, pp. 131–188. The University of Chicago Press.

- Janvier, Philippe. 1996, 2003. Early Vertebrates (1996); Early Vertebrates (2003). Oxford Monographs on Geology and Geophysics, v. 33, Oxford University Press, Oxford, England, ISBN 978-0-19-854047-2

- Jiang, Pan, and Wang Shi-tao. "New finding of Galeaspiformes in South China." *Acta Palaeontologica Sinica* 19.1 (1980): 1-7.

- Jørgensen, Jørgen Mørup, et al., eds. *The biology of hagfishes*. Springer Science & Business Media, 2012.

- Long, John A. *The Rise of Fishes: 500 Million Years of Evolution*. Baltimore: The Johns Hopkins University Press, 1996

- Sansom IJ, Smith MP, Smith MM and Turner P (1997) "*Astraspis*: The anatomy and histology of an Ordovician fish" Palaeontology, 40 (3): 625–642.

- Sansom, Robert S. "Phylogeny, classification and character polarity of the Osteostraci (Vertebrata)." *Journal of Systematic Palaeontology* 7.1 (2009): 95-115.

- Sansom, Robert S; Kim Freedman; Sarah E Gabbott; Richard J. Aldridge; Mark A. Purnell (2010). "Taphonomy and Affinity of an Enigmatic Silurian Vertebrate, Jamoytius Kerwoodi White". *Palaeontology*. **53** (6): 1393–1409

- Soehn, K. L., Märss, T., Caldwell, M. W. & Wilson, M. V. H., 2001: New and biostratigraphically useful thelodonts from the Silurian of the Mackenzie Mountains, Northwest Territories, Canada. Journal of Vertebrate Paleontology, 21: 651-659

- Turner, Susan. Thelodus Macintoshi Stetson 1928: The Largest Known Thelodont (Agnatha: Thelodonti). Museum of Comparative Zoology, 1986.
- White, E. I. "On Cephalaspis lyelli Agassiz." *Palaeontology* 1.2 (1958): 99-105.
- Young, G.C. 1991: The first armoured agnathan vertebrates from the Devonian of Australia. Pp. 67-85 in: Chang, M-M.; Liu, Y-H.; Zhang, G.-R. (eds.), Early vertebrates and related problems of evolutionary biology. Science Press, Beijing, China.
- Zhu, Min, and Zhikun Gai. "Phylogenetic relationships of galeaspids (Agnatha)." *Frontiers of Biology in China* 2.2 (2007): 151-169.

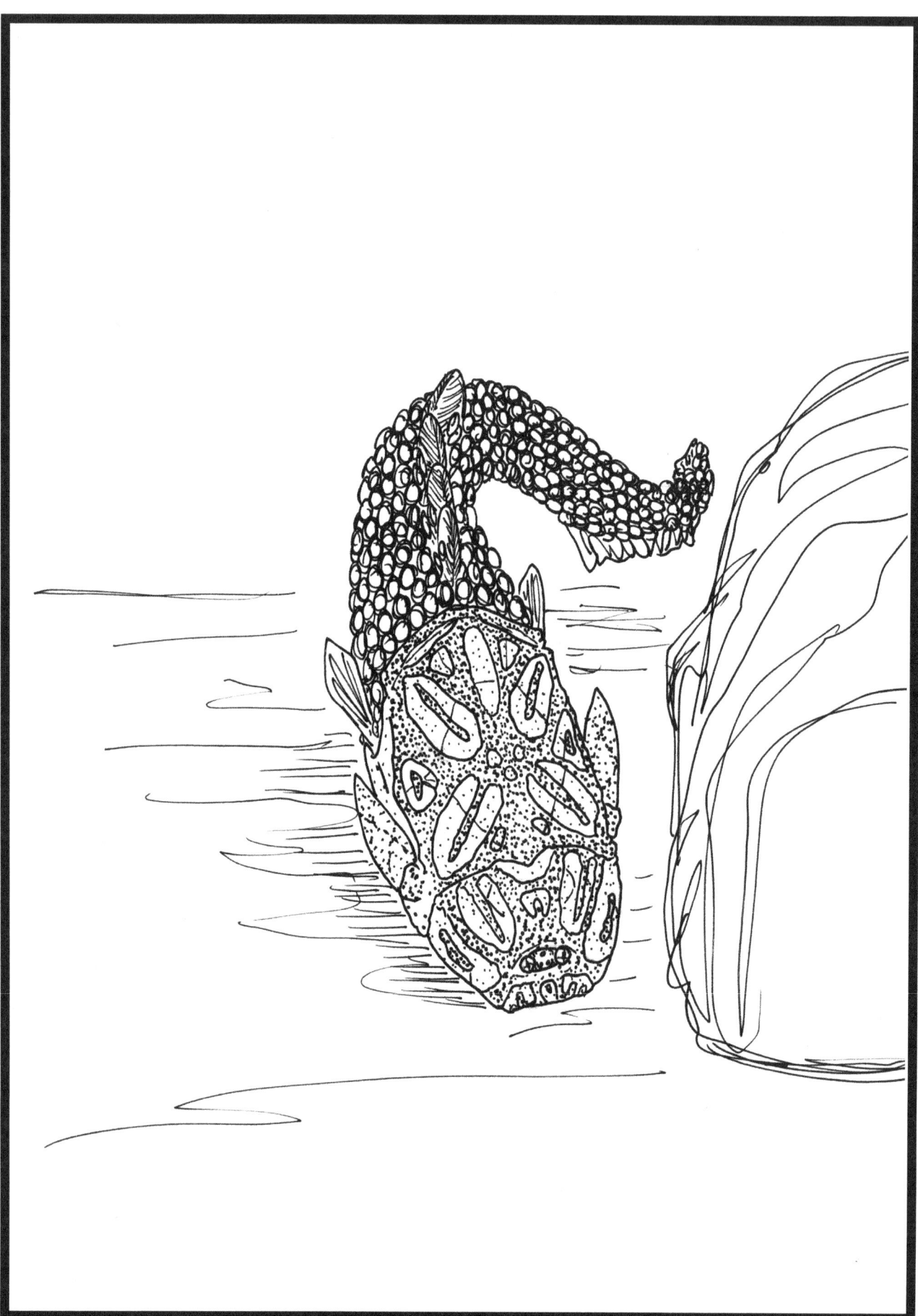

About the Artist

Stanton F. Fink is a student of Biology and Chinese Medicine, and makes a hobby of drawing monsters and researching flowers, arcane-looking creatures, prehistoric animals, fish, reptiles, birds and the occasional, really grotesque fungal fruiting body.

Stanton grew up and went to school in California and is currently living, drawing, and gardening in Oregon.

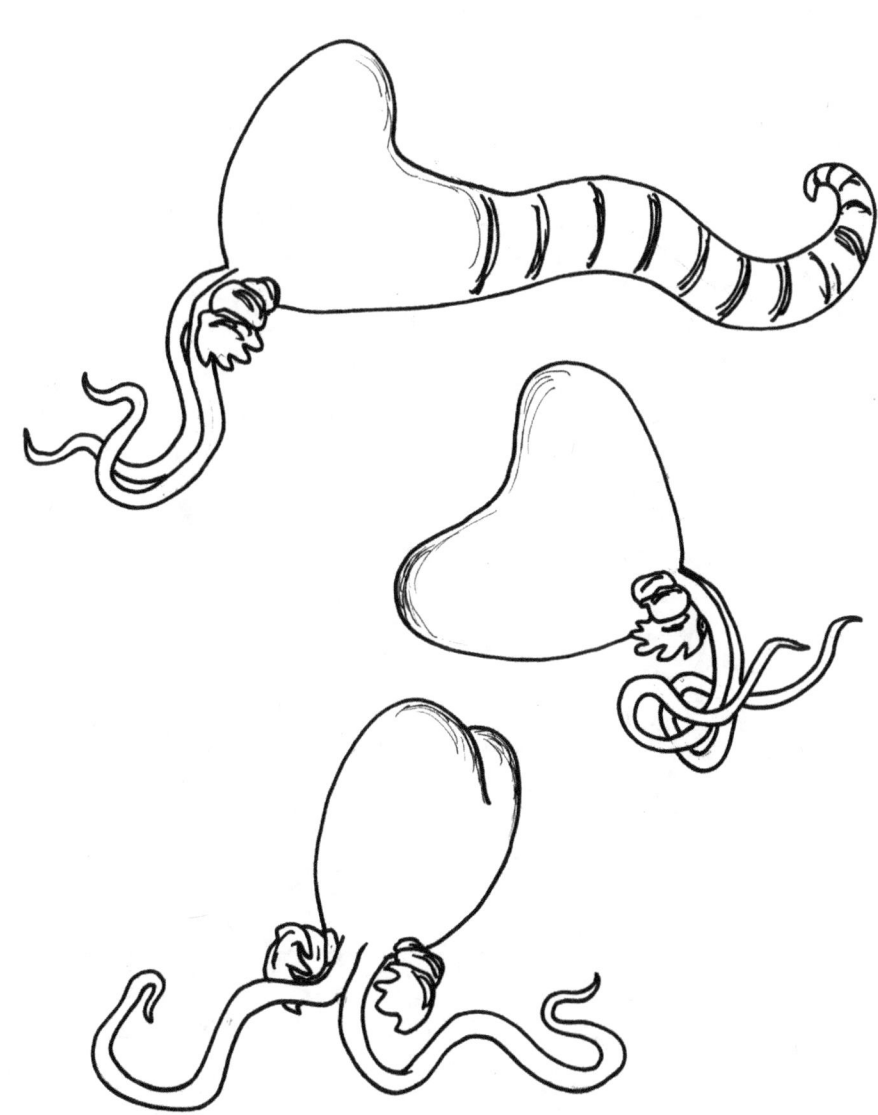

www.ingramcontent.com/pod-product-compliance
Lightning Source LLC
Chambersburg PA
CBHW081758280526
45789CB00008B/2902